CURIOUS KIDS DISCOVER CAROLINA BIRDS

ANOTHER IN THE SERIES OF:
THE ADVENTURES OF SIMPLY SAM

**Written By:
Jim Eberwein**

Copyright© 2019 by Jim Eberwein.
All rights reserved.

Illustrations Copyright© 2019 by COT Publishing.
All rights reserved.

ISBN-13: 9781677807512

All rights reserved. This work may not be reproduced in any form, in whole or in part, without written permission from the author. For written permission to reproduce selections from this book, write to COT Publishing, P. O. Box 3379 Myrtle Beach, South Carolina 29578.

Available from Amazon.com, and other retail outlets

I would like to dedicate this book to my loving wife Carole, who, without her support and encouragement I would not have been able to produce this book.

In addition, I would also like to dedicate this book to a little boy called Joey, who, only 5 years old, took a liking to an old man, while drinking his iced tea and eating a donut at Dunkin. Joey teaches me new things, that I can use in my books, every time I see him.

Section 1 Land Birds

Birds

 Belted Kingfisher

 Brown Thrasher

 Carolina Chickadee

 Eastern Kingbird

 Hooded Warbler

 Red-Bellied Woodpecker

Belted Kingfisher

Image by David Mark from Pixabay

Land Birds of the Carolinas

Belted Kingfisher male birds are blue-gray and have a white collar with a gray band on their belly. The female birds are also blue-gray, but have a chestnut colored band on their belly and top of their legs.

They live near small streams of water, ponds, rivers and lakes. Their nests are dug into soft banks near water. They sit on high tree branches and phone lines and dive into shallow water for fish, frogs and other small water animals. They spend winters where it doesn't freeze so they can find food.

Their square-tipped tails are medium in length and when flying their wings open up to two feet. They weigh almost one and a half pounds.

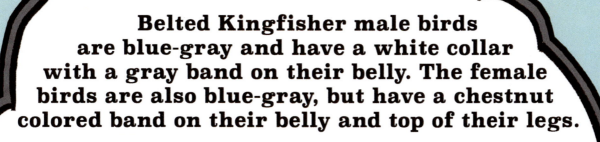

Sam

Willy

Brown Thrasher

Photo by Jeff Jones from Free Images

Land Birds of the Carolinas

Carolina Chickadee

Image by anne773 from Pixabay

Land Birds of the Carolinas

Eastern Kingbird

Image by Ray Miller from Pixabay

Land Birds of the Carolinas

Doesn't this bird look like a King the way he holds himself on the stump? They have a body which is grayish black on its wings and back and a white belly and chin. Their head is a darker black than their back and wings. The tip of their tails are white.

Kingbirds do have a crown but keep it hidden under their head feathers most of the time. The crown has yellow, orange and red feathers. When the birds are hunting food or chasing other birds away, they sometimes show the crown and open their beaks very wide showing a red throat, and then dive at the other birds or food.

The birds mate in open areas like yards, fields and places along the edges of forests and water. The female bird will sit on the eggs for up to 18 days. The young birds will take their first flight in about 16 to 18 days from the time the eggs hatch.

Luis

Hooded Warbler

Image by psnaturephotography from iStock

Land Birds of the Carolinas

> These are one of the prettiest birds in the Carolinas. They are olive green on their wings and backs with black hoods and throats and yellow foreheads and cheeks. Their bellies are also a bright yellow. They have large black eyes. The female bird does not have the black hood. The birds fly between shrubs flashing their white outer tail feathers.
> They normally stay hidden in heavy bushes in the forest, jumping up to eat insects or grabbing them from the leaves.

> The individual male Hooded Warbler sings slightly different songs and learn to recognize their neighbor birds by their songs. They can tell if it's friendly, or not, and know if they have to defend their area.

Sophia

Max

Red-Bellied Woodpecker

Image by skeeze from Pixabay

Land Birds of the Carolinas

These birds do not really have red bellies. They have red flecks on their white belly and that's how they got their name. They do have red heads and white cheeks. Their backs and wings are striped black and white. When they fly, you might see white patches near their wing tips. They are common in many Carolina forests and also appear at backyard bird-feeders. They eat suet, peanuts and sometimes sunflower seeds. The birds can stick out their tongues almost two inches from the end of their beaks. The tips of their tongue are spiky, and the bird spit is sticky, so it is easier to get food from deep cracks.

The woodpeckers eats insects and small spiders. They will also eat items like acorns, nuts and seeds from plants that grow every year. They also like grapes and oranges.

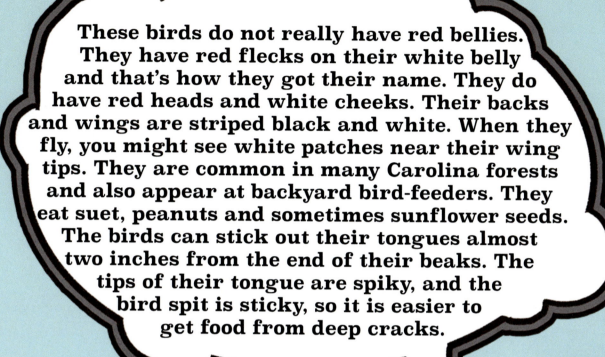

Aki

Section 2 Coastal Birds

Birds

 Brown Pelican

 Common Tern

 Laughing Gull

 American Oystercatcher

 Willet

 Red Knot

Brown Pelican

Photo by Fred McWilson from Free Images

Coastal Birds of the Carolinas

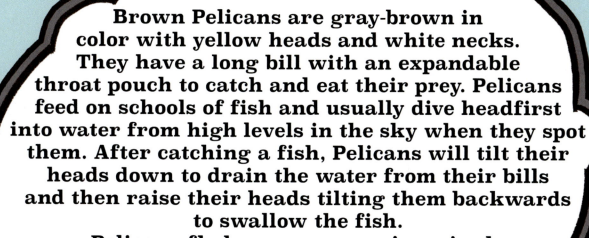

Brown Pelicans are gray-brown in color with yellow heads and white necks. They have a long bill with an expandable throat pouch to catch and eat their prey. Pelicans feed on schools of fish and usually dive headfirst into water from high levels in the sky when they spot them. After catching a fish, Pelicans will tilt their heads down to drain the water from their bills and then raise their heads tilting them backwards to swallow the fish.
Pelicans fly low over waves in a single file and sometimes in a V-shape formation like geese. They will fly near buildings along the coast to take advantage of the air currents.

Pelicans build nests out of grass, twigs and sticks in low shrubs and small trees. They nest in groups or colonies. The male bird gets the nest material and the female builds the nest.

Sam

Common Tern

Photo by Julia Soininen from Free Images

Coastal Birds of the Carolinas

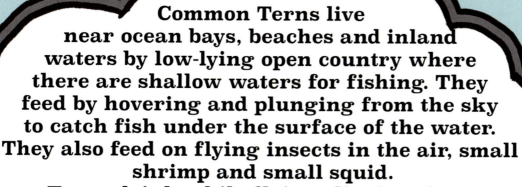

Common Terns live near ocean bays, beaches and inland waters by low-lying open country where there are shallow waters for fishing. They feed by hovering and plunging from the sky to catch fish under the surface of the water. They also feed on flying insects in the air, small shrimp and small squid.

Terns drink while flying, dipping their bill into the water with their wings held high. They can drink either saltwater or fresh water. When mating, the males may fly over a colony of terns carrying a fish in their bill with females following them. On the ground, the birds face each other bowing and strutting (moving) in circles. The males then give the fish to the females.

Nest sites for the Common Terns are usually on the ground or by low shrubs or foliage (undergrowth).

Seiko

Laughing Gull

Image by Paul Brennan from Pixabay

Coastal Birds of the Carolinas

Laughing Gulls nest along beaches in salt-marshes, on islands and in mangroves. They form colonies of up to 25,000 pairs and sometimes join other kinds of birds such as terns, larger gulls and American Oystercatchers.

They eat many different things. They like earthworms, insects, snails, crabs and crab eggs. They also eat garbage and discards from fishing boats. They look for food while walking, wading or swimming or by diving into water. Sometimes, they hover over the heads of pelicans that have just caught a fish trying to get the fish to slip out of the pelican's bill.

The gulls place their nests on sand, rocks and mats of dead plants or hide them underneath leaves of low plants. Both the males and females build the nests. The males sometimes begin building the nests to attract the females. They continue to bring material, but the females arrange the nest. The males and females may stay together for several breeding seasons.

Jamir

American Oystercatcher

Photo by luis rock from Free Images

Coastal Birds of the Carolinas

American Oystercatchers are interesting birds. Their heads and necks are black, and their wings and backs are dark brown with white patches that can be seen when the birds are flying. Their chests and bellies are white, and they have bright red bills and pink feet.

They feed on oysters. That is where they got their name. When the birds find an open oyster, they put their long bill into the oyster cutting the muscles that are used to close the shell of the oyster. The inside of the oyster is then easily eaten. They also eat clams, mussels, snail's, fiddler crabs and other small insects that live in saltwater.

Nesting begins in April and ends in July. They nest on mounds of washed oyster shells. Breeding males and females can be seen running side by side with their heads low while making loud noises near their nesting site. Each bird sits on the eggs for about a month.

Emma

Willet

Image by Nature-Pix from Pixabay

Coastal Birds of the Carolinas

These birds have spotted brown feathers when breeding and gray colors in the winter. When they are flying you can see a bold white and black stripe going the length of each wing. They have long straight bills that are a dark color. Their tails are short and square. Willets in the Carolinas have fatter bills and more spotting on their backs and chests than birds in the west.
Willets find food with not just their eyes, but by using the tips of their sensitive bills. Because their bills are sensitive, they can feed both during the day and night.
Willets are usually seen feeding alone. They are deliberate when they walk and stop to dig for crabs, worms and other food with their bills. When scared, they make a sharp noise, open their wings and run rather than fly.

Willets breed and nest in salt-marshes and barrier islands along the Carolinas. Their nests will be in salt-grass and beach-grass and on sand dunes or in short grass on barrier dunes. After chicks are born, the female leaves the nest two weeks before the male, leaving him to finish raising the chicks.

Sophia

Red Knot

Image by Public DomainImages from Pixabay

Coastal Birds of the Carolinas

Sam: Red Knots nest in the far north and breed in the Arctic Circle. They migrate to South Carolina and live and nest on islands along the coast. During the migration, they eat clams and Horseshoe Crab eggs when the crabs come on shore to spawn. The birds are large and stocky and have orange bellies and chests with gold, buff and red coloring. They have black backs and wings. Their bills are medium length and they have short legs.

Max: They feed by sight but also by putting their bills into the sand. When they eat small mollusks, they swallow them whole and their stomach muscles crush the shells. They also eat clams, mussels and their larvae. When they clean themselves, they cover their feathers with a protective wax by touching a "preening gland" and then their feathers. They rest by lying on their bellies.

Section 3 Raptors

Birds

 Bald Eagle

 Turkey Vulture

 Red Shouldered Hawk

 Great Horned Owl

 Osprey

 Peregrine Falcon

Bald Eagle

Image by skeeze from Pixabay

Raptors of the Carolinas

Turkey Vulture

Image by skeeze from Pixabay

Raptors of the Carolinas

Red Shouldered Hawk

Image by skeeze from Pixabay

Raptors of the Carolinas

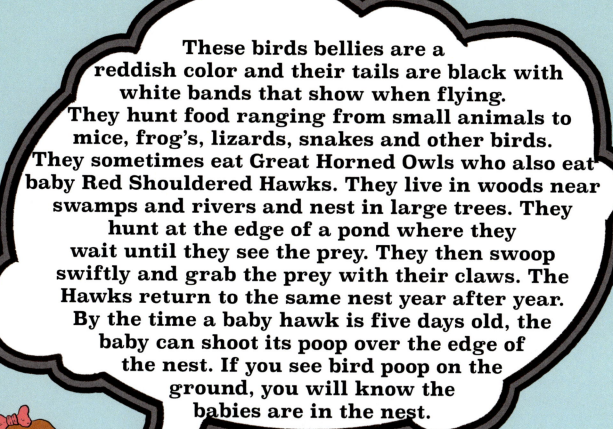

These birds bellies are a reddish color and their tails are black with white bands that show when flying. They hunt food ranging from small animals to mice, frog's, lizards, snakes and other birds. They sometimes eat Great Horned Owls who also eat baby Red Shouldered Hawks. They live in woods near swamps and rivers and nest in large trees. They hunt at the edge of a pond where they wait until they see the prey. They then swoop swiftly and grab the prey with their claws. The Hawks return to the same nest year after year. By the time a baby hawk is five days old, the baby can shoot its poop over the edge of the nest. If you see bird poop on the ground, you will know the babies are in the nest.

Sophia

Great Horned Owl

Image by H Maria from Pixabay

Raptors of the Carolinas

Look at those ears! Are they big? What about those eyes? These owls also have a hooting voice and are one of the most common owls in the Carolinas. They also are very aggressive hunters that can attack other raptors such as Ospreys, Peregrine Falcons, and other Owls. They will also eat other smaller animals, frogs, mice and scorpions. These Owls have large yellow eyes with dark centers that open very wide in the dark, which helps them see at night. Their eyes do not move in their sockets but the owls can move their head 180 degrees so they can look in any direction. They also have sensitive hearing which helps them hunt at night.

When these Owls have caught their prey and closed their claws, it can take up to 28 pounds of force to open a claw. They use their claws (or talons) to cut the spine of their larger prey.

Sam

Osprey

Image by WikiImages from Pixabay

Raptors of the Carolinas

Ospreys are very large birds. They have long narrow wings and long legs. They fly with a bend in their wings. They are brown on their backs and white on their bellies and legs. Their heads are white with a brown stripe around their eyes. Ospreys can be seen near bodies of water (rivers, ponds, reservoirs) and on the Intracoastal Waterway in the Carolinas. They are seen flying over the waterway and their nests are in trees and on channel marker platforms along the shore and in the water. Their nests are huge and made of sticks with bark and sod on the inside.

Their main food is fish and they dive feet first when getting a fish. Their claws have a reversible outer toe that allows them to hold fish with two toes in front and behind. They also have barbs (little hooks) on the bottoms of their feet. This allows the bird to hold slippery fish . They line up the fish head first when flying. This cuts down the wind resistance and makes it easier to fly holding the fish.

Aki

Peregrine Falcon

Image by jasmin777 from Pixabay

Raptors of the Carolinas

These birds are fast-flying birds. They hunt medium-sized shorebirds and ducklings. They are very good at catching pigeons, striking them from high above. They can fly normally from 25 to 34 miles per hour (mph) when chasing food. At times they can reach speeds up to 69mph. When diving toward another bird from high above, they may reach a speed of 200mph. That is fast. The Peregrine Falcon is the largest of the falcons. They have long pointed wings and long tails. They are blue gray on their backs with a vertically striped belly and chest and black head with white around the beak.

When falcons go after birds, they may swoop from 300 to 3000 feet above the prey. They will either grab the prey or strike it with their feet to stun or kill it. The Falcons then grab the prey with their beak and bite it through the neck to kill it.

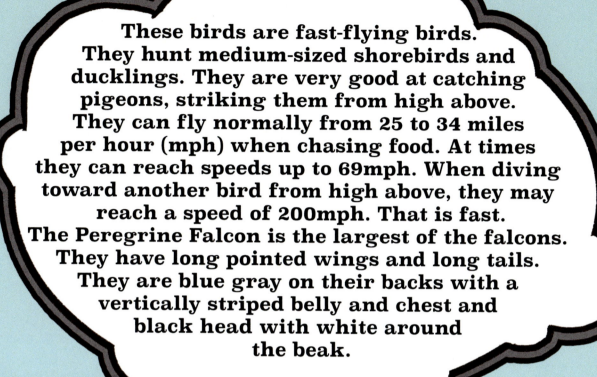

Jamir

Section 4 Wading Birds

Birds

 Great Egret

 Snowy Egret

 Wood Stork

 Yellow Crowned Night Heron

 Great Blue Heron

 Roseate Spoonbill

Great Egret

Image by skeeze from Pixabay

Wading Birds of the Carolinas

These birds are tall and have a yellow-orange bill and black legs. Their body is all white. When they fly, their legs are bent, and their neck is bent back against their shoulders. They fly slowly with a cruising speed around 25 mph. They eat fish, crabs, crayfish and insects and can be found near ponds, reservoirs, lakes and rivers. They need daylight in order to find their food and wait for their prey to come to them. They find their prey by seeing them in the water and then strike and catch their prey with their bill and swallow them.

The Great Egrets nest in colonies or groups and prefer older trees with horizontal limbs that may be up to 100 feet from the ground. In the breeding season, a patch on the Great Egret's face turns green and long curls (plumes) grow on their back. When young hatch in the nest, they fight between themselves and many times the larger chicks will kill the smaller siblings.

Sam

Snowy Egret

Image by Susan Frazier from Pixabay

Wading Birds of the Carolinas

These birds are medium-sized and have a body that is white with dark legs and greenish-yellow feet. Their bills are black with a bit of yellow near their head. In the 1800's, the Snowy Egrets feathers were worth more money than gold. The birds were killed for their beautiful feathers (plumes) to be used in the fashion industry for hats. They nest in groups like the Great Egret, usually on protected islands. You will find them in mudflats, beaches and wetland areas in thick vegetation. They sometimes will mix with other wading birds. The Snowy Egret aggressively defend their nests. The predators that go after them are raccoons, Great Horned Owls, crows, snakes, and crocodiles.

They eat mainly water animals such as fish, frogs, worms and insects. When they are looking for food, they walk and sometimes run in shallow water. They also will stand still waiting for prey to approach. They might stir the bottom with their feet to surprise their prey and make them move so they can grab them with their bill.

Sophia

Wood Stork

Image by Paul Brennan from Pixabay

Wading Birds of the Carolinas

Wood Storks are the biggest wading bird breeding in South Carolina. They have bald black necks and heads with white bodies and black tails. The wing feathers are black on the underside which show in flight. The Wood Storks, when flying, extend their necks and legs unlike herons and egrets. When they perch, they pull their necks in, so they look hump backed. This bird hunts differently than herons and egrets. It hunts by feeling for fish, shrimp, crayfish and other prey. They go through shallow water with their bills open sweeping back and forth. They also move their feet up and down to scare the prey. When they sense a prey with their bill, it snaps shut and catches the prey.

These birds also nest in colonies in higher branches of cypress or black gum trees, which are in standing water. This keeps them away from predators. There could be up to 25 nests in one tree. When it is hot and there are chicks in the nest, the parent birds throw-up on the chicks to keep them cool.

Luis

Yellow Crowned Night Heron

Photo by Thomas Pate from FreeImages

Wading Birds of the Carolinas

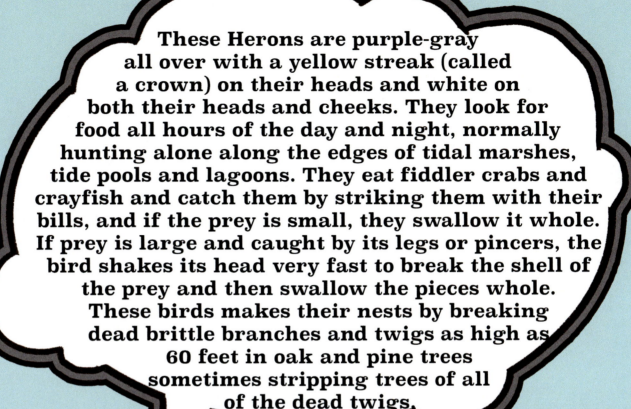

These Herons are purple-gray all over with a yellow streak (called a crown) on their heads and white on both their heads and cheeks. They look for food all hours of the day and night, normally hunting alone along the edges of tidal marshes, tide pools and lagoons. They eat fiddler crabs and crayfish and catch them by striking them with their bills, and if the prey is small, they swallow it whole. If prey is large and caught by its legs or pincers, the bird shakes its head very fast to break the shell of the prey and then swallow the pieces whole. These birds makes their nests by breaking dead brittle branches and twigs as high as 60 feet in oak and pine trees sometimes stripping trees of all of the dead twigs.

They are normally found in wetland barrier islands, salt-marshes, swamps and drainage ditches. The heron pair nest alone but sometimes in colonies of several hundred pairs. Some of these sites will stay in use for up to 20 years. **WOW!!!**

Alexis

Great Blue Heron

Photo by Jeff Jones from Free Images

Wading Birds of the Carolinas

These birds are mostly blue-gray with white on their heads and cheeks. They also have a white streak down their neck. They move slowly, but the Herons can strike their prey in a lightning move to grab it for food. They are the largest Herons in North America and weigh only 5 to 6 pounds because they have hollow bones. They have long legs, sinuous necks and thick orange and white dagger like bills. These birds have special feathers on their chests. They grow all the time and fray. The Herons brush these feathers with a fringed claw on their middle toe. This claw, along with the special feathers help remove the oil and slime from the feathers and apply a powder to their underbelly to protect them from the swamp oil and slime.

Great Blue Herons live in both fresh and saltwater locations. They have been found to mostly eat fish that are sick and would soon die. These sick fish are usually near the surface of the water and are easier to catch. Herons can also hunt by day or night. They have special receptors in their eyes that give them their improved night vision.

Emma

Roseate Spoonbill

Photo by luis rock from FreeImages

Wading Birds of the Carolinas

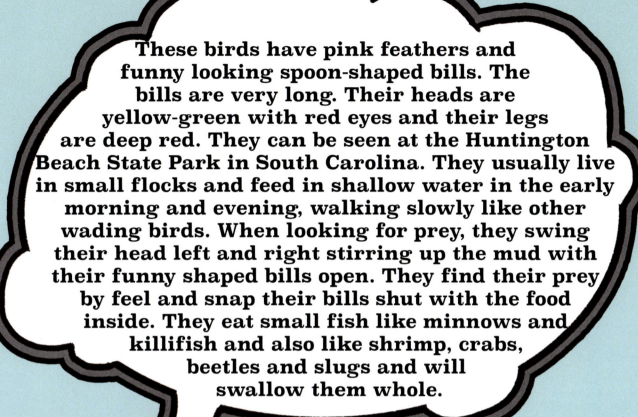

Acknowledgments

I want to thank the Coastal Authors Network for taking the time to review my book and offer their constructive criticism. They have been a great help in putting this book together.

I would also like to thank my illustrator jjawzip on fiverr.com. He is located in the Philippines and has been fantastic in developing the characters I use to describe the birds. He has taken my ideas and projected them visually for everyone to see. He's great. I used these characters to design each of the pages of the book.

I also want to thank my wife for supporting me during the time it has taken me to write this book. Without her support, I would never have been able to complete this project.

In addition, I would like to thank Lucy and Tom Moore of Lucy's Toys for giving me permission to use the image of one of their hand puppets (Stomper B/W) for my character Maximillian (Max). You can see all of their other creations at www.lucystoys.com.

The following images used in my book were provided by Images by Clker-Free-Vector-Images from Pixabay. They are: Joey, Wally, Bella, the bird sketch on the page with Alexis, the Vulture sketch on the page with Luis, the Bald Eagle sketch on the page with Max, the Hawk sketch on the page with Sophia, the Grass on each page and the Bird sketches on the Title Page.

Acknowlements (Cont'd)

References and Sources

The following is a list of references and sources I used in gathering the information on birds included in this book. For further information about each of the birds shown in the book, please go to the websites listed.

1) American Bird Conservancy
   www.abcbirds.org/bird/(name of bird)
2) Audubon Guide to North American Birds
   www.audubon.org/field-guide/bird-guide
3) Birds of North Carolina
   www.ncbirds.carolinabirdclub.org
4) National Geographic
   www.nationalgeographic.com.animals.birds.(name of bird)
5) NatureMapping Foundation
   www.naturemappingfoundation.org/natmap/facts/(name of bird)
6) North Carolina Department of Natural and Cultural Resources
   www.ncdcr.gov
7) North Carolina Wildlife Federation
   www.ncwf.org
8) Smithsonian National Zoo
   www.nationalzoo.sl.edu/animals/(name of bird)
9) South Carolina Department of Natural Resources
   www.dnr.sc.gov/birds
10) The Cornell Lab of Ornithology
    www.allaboutbirds.org
11) The National Wildlife Federation
    www. nwf.org/Education-Resources/Wildlife-Guide/Birds/(name of bird)
12) Wikipedia
    www.wikipedia.org/wiki/(name of bird)

About The Author

Jim Eberwein is the grandfather of twenty-two who reside in North Carolina, Massachusetts and Rhode Island. He has traveled the world as a Business/Industry Consultant and lived in the United States, Mexico, England and Russia. His extensive travel and experience with many grandchildren has helped him to develop many stories, adventures and informational books that young minds will enjoy.

In this book Jim has used his main character, Sam and his friends from other books he wrote, to describe some of the many birds that live in the Carolinas. He hopes you enjoy the information provided and take the opportunity to learn more using the references and source websites he has provided. Enjoy and learn.

Made in the USA
Columbia, SC
15 January 2022